Spare Change for the Crossing

Spare Change for the Crossing / Last Poems © Peter Weltner 2023

ISBN: 979-8-218-31417-0

Marrowstoner Press

Spare Change for the Crossing

Last Poems

Peter Weltner

What images return
O my daughter.

T.S. Eliot, "Marina"

To the Memory of Tom Johnston from L.A.
and Our One Night Together
in Early Fall, 1971

A shepherd chances on a forgotten, archaic
king's tomb dug into a hillside
of the Peloponnese, the walls thick,
the earth rich with shards and treasures he'll hide
by leaving them where he found them: a golden greave,
scattered pottery, a battered shield embossed with a hero's story.
He'll never return, vows never to retrieve
such precious things, his only chance for wealth and glory.
A diver hired at great expense discovers
a bronze kouros lying in mud at the bottom
of the sea in murky waters
churned by tides, but swears to his patrons it was a phantom
they saw, no more than sun's rays fathoms
deep playing like moonlight on a temple's marble columns.

Table of Contents

IV.

I

Three Poems after Euripides
for Patricia McCarthy

Part One

Orest

I have seen men kill, entire families slay each other.
I have swum in brutal seas past coastal shelfs bent,
worn, jagged, riptides clashing. I have watched waves smother
sailors dying tangled in beds of kelp. I went
away for a while, fled home as a storm
howled in my ears, buried bodies in a field of flowers.
Nightmares are the form
life takes when it burrows into the dark of caves. A boy cowers
in my arms. A girl flees
from me unable to bear what she sees.
A wolf kills to eat.
A hawk, a shark must destroy to survive.
But men are worse than beasts, raw, the play incomplete,
no one left at the end alive.

I remember my mother shrieking like waves breaking
on cliffs, like Odysseus weeping about
the wife he left behind, abandoning
his honor, his peace of mind, then lashing out
at her suitors, her handmaids without sorrow,
feeling no pity
for those he had murdered. Tomorrow,
Delphi, cheating, deceiving me
of what the unquiet dead bestow
on the guilty. In a field of flowers,
redder than blood where I rage below
against their watchful eyes, roars,
like the machinery of wars, the furies,
avengers, killers of men, destroyers of cities.

Part Two

The Andromache

1. Andromache's Farewell

Three times Achilles dragged my husband
round our sacred city
unbinding it from Apollo
and his protection. Now I understand
why gods' promises are hollow,
lacking all pity.
They want my son, me
to perish. He is a swallow in a hawk's nest,
I a coney in a lair of wolves.
I fear the lasciviousness of Greeks. I detest
them and their wars. My child pulls
at my hair, protesting my tears.
While Troy burns to the ground, I know he must die:
a fledgling flung from his roost when too young to fly.

2. Andromache's Lament

Like a fury, I'd hasten after his soul's
descent. A red
fire glows
over the city's walls and towers. The dead
see more than the reviled
ones like me, the soon to be killed or exiled.
They watch me moan and cry
because I cannot bear to watch you die,
Astyanax. Whose child is this
I have kidnapped instead, my heart like stone?
In the presence of the rampaging Greeks, let me kiss
him as if he were my own,
my child though no son of Hector,
and I, his murderer, wailing louder than his true mother.

3. Andromache in Phthia

Myths. Lies. Those stories composing my legend. My son is dead.
Another son lives unsafely on, Molussus, scion
of Achilles through Neoptolemus, whom rumors have said
is my lover. Why won't I admit it? I watch a stream run
up to the temple's columns, then flee
back to the sea, pearl-pure in its nacreous beauty.
Childless, barren Hermione,
fiancée to my boyfriend, would kill me if she could. No good
ever comes from a royal's jealousy.
The bitch berates me like a high queen secure
in her birthright, blood-
lust pouring from her tear-reddened eyes, cocksure
of her rights and duty as she stands before me, struting,
preening, defaming me, calling me names: 'Barbarian,' 'Whore,' 'Trojan Slut.'

4. Andromache on Helen

Let Helen never sleep soundly, her heart the foulest, most impure,
vulgarest of the Greeks. My husband was the prize
the gods awarded them for their cruelty, their pillaging nature,
their ferocity. My life has become one disguise
after another. Literature
tries me, condemns me for the child who dies
thrown off a wall over and over again in its pages, a boy my own
or another mother's. Or mourns, laments with me. Whole tragedies
have been written about that one scene, though I alone
know the facts of what happened or once thought I did
while I was there, the one true witness. I am no longer sure
of my history. To bear children is tragic. Any other truth is hidden
from me, as dark as Zeus. Or Helen, passionate Helen, lascivious
and erotic, divinity, a lesser Aphrodite, seductive, doomed, and perfidious.

5. Andromache Appeals to Thetis

Now Neoptolemus has been beaten, defeated, too,
abused, murdered. Seducer, rapist, my savior,
which of the three was he? I leave it to the future
to decide. I must bear
his loss alone. Sanctity
is far rarer, more precious than beauty.
Let Thetis appear to me,
Nereid,
demigoddess of the sea.
I must be wed
again, though I have died many times at the brute hands
and lusts of men. By her shrine, near land's
end, I wait for her to rise, more frightening than Hector
gazing at me as I washed his wounds and bloodstained armor.

6. Andromache in Molossia

Tragedy is never reasonable. Always circuitous, it twists
and turns, then aims its arrows to shatter
us, like the dark matter
of the universe, what no one can resist.
Picture me, if you can, as an old Trojan matron
wearing a gold embroidered shawl,
costly possessions scattered about me, finest hand woven
tapestries, delicate pottery, gleaming mosaics on every wall
portraying our victories. A pretty image in a way, isn't it?, a fine old age
for Andromache with Helenus who made, Virgil wrote, a new Troy
in Molossia. Yet daily I continue to rage
against my fate, grow no wiser, suffer like an animal, know no joy,
forced to hear in my ears the monstrous din
of epic wars and the cries of my city's dying children.

Part Three

Medea

He said he loved me. I gave him all my savage magic.
That is the heart of tragedy. He said he would stay
with me. But he abandoned me for her. Made me sick
with jealousy. I begged him, "Don't go. Don't betray
me." But he found her waiting in her walled city. Say
I am too much the man, though I grieve like a sorceress
wearing a black shawl of mourning on her long way back
up mountains to olive groves where the oldest goddesses
dwell among the smell of sweet fruit under looming black
summer suns. Demeter, I'd say, Hecate, teach me to live
in sorrow, to sing my threnodies full-voiced and angry as I thrill
to his fingers on my willing, impassioned body. Dreams, give
him to me, his lips, hands, prick, calves for me to kiss. He is my tragic
inevitability, the way a war is, or so they say. The cities we ruin. The people we kill.

θάλασσα/Thalassa/The Sea

1.

When Stefan went mad, he slowly stepped on rocks
along the sea terrified that he'd fall through
the gaps between them into the Absolute. Flocks
of pelicans in their strict formation are flying to

the headlands northwest. The beach is a cemetery,
broken grave markers, the Prince Philip's hull,
shattered shells, buried fin whales, driftwood, sea-
weed, jellyfish baking in the sun. He is trying to cull

from it what might save him, lugging a rucksack
for refuse over his shoulders. Dawn is too new
to cast enough light between Stef and the crack
in the earth he fears. He prefers to die with eyes open, true

to his life, his sights set on the view on Tam's summit
of the Pacific from the make-do lookout tower
of the storm-bent oak he'll climb soon—infinite, no limit
to what he can know of the sea's undertows below its surging water.

2.

Breaking hard on dunes, the heavy waves portend catastrophe.
No one can sleep, listening to them crash.   At dawn,
a semen-white, viscous foam churns up from the sea
and floats over the sand, blown by winds. The spawn
of life from waves grinding the land.
The storm has littered the beach with relics.

It is strange how the meaning of things is reserved for specifics.
A strand of claspless costume pearls.
A pair of dark gray argyll socks.
Ripped black jeans, likely a girl's.
A pile of tangled seaweed and moss-encrusted rocks.
Sticks of driftwood. Fish hooks bound with a rubber band.

Last night, the stars in the Milky Way flickered with a red or sea-blue
aura as if premonitory of the storm to come, hurricane-strong, while you
told me how you loved me, how you could trace it in my face like lines in the sand.

3.

Fragments, remnants of ancient writings, glyphs, like glimpses
of the past left for the future to interpret, corrupt faded texts,
whose meanings are lost, randomly tossed like tempest blown leaves.
Myths with so many gaps between words what happens next

is forever forgotten. Unknown voyages on unmapped seas.
Uncharted journeys through waterless wastelands.
Hearts, souls of the dead weathered nameless on dried hides,
parchment shredding in pots hidden in caves or desert sands.

Runes, inscriptions of heroic conquests, marauding tribes
riding down from the north, legends chiseled in stone. Bodies
laden with gold laid in ships that sailed through distant waters,
stripped of flesh by currents. Polished whiter than moonlit

snow, bones of heroes no longer riding the sea, roaming for plunder,
no more hoarding, no more coastal searching for signs of harbor,
longhouses, wives, plentiful mead. On bits of papyrus, signs
of desires, unhealed wounds, old sorrows and loves that rhyme

with ours, we think. Panta rei, Herakleitos said. The sea of things
flows like rivers. Like fires endlessly kindled and extinguished,
it burns. Maybe it is true (is time a liar like us?) that nothing's
lost if we could learn how to comprehend the language of the dead.

4.

Tomorrow, the crew will sail on a calm Mediterranean Sea,
the sky blue, sun bronze, sand white as wind
unless a storm comes to blow the ship on an odyssey
to unknown lands or an island unrecorded on a map.
Their captain smiles, pleased by who his sailors are,
reckless and brave as he is. Only mortal failings can trap
them in a port, fearful of voyaging off course, far
from Greece to where the sun sets over mountain peaks
in the east and men rise from slumbering beneath the sea
to warn the living of what dangers await, enticing as a siren's
song. Tonight, the ship's lights flare on the water. The sea
is beautiful, as if flaming white and yellow, sparkling like men's
eyes beholding the moon. For a few more hours, the ship rests in a harbor
artful as the gods the city worships, embodied in herm, façade, kouros, and column.

Colonus

Beyond a dense stand of scrub pine and olive trees,
a grove waits for him, his eyes moon-luminous
and white as his robes, darkness all he sees
as he wanders deeper in, unsure of the way, curious

why he has been called there and by whom. Soon
he might know. As a boy, he'd seen tiny, translucent,
eyeless fish swimming in a pool no cloudless noon
had ever shone upon in a dank, underground cave, sent

there, he guessed, as an omen to save for the end
of his days. The dead need not see to satisfy
their hunger, or might see blindingly, content
to be without vision and all it seems to portend

of sorrow and misery. Is this what it means to die?
To walk without knowing where he's going or why
into a strange grove where, at the sound of thunder
he'll disappear, forever free of fear, into the wide-eyed wonder
    of earth and air and water?

Clytemnestra

In the Peloponnesus, in Mycenae, try to imagine the stone walls,
iron gates, gold masks, hidden bronze doors now lost
to history, its palace's narrow, ghost-haunted halls,
cliffs behind it where water poured off rock frost-
pale in the morning cold, and the enormous marble fountain
that bore purifying water from the sacred mountain
whose hillsides hid the spirits of those who had died
among its sacred leaves, vines, and outcrops hazy
in the mist at dawn.
                       Agamemnon will die, too, who has lied,
her husband, from kingly pride all his cruel life.
                                   Yet Clytemnestra's baby,
her sole son, last night was a coiling snake she tried
to feed with her breast until it bit her and curdled
her milk. Her scream as she woke at once alerted
her sleeping guards.
                       Guilty dreams fly into and out of her mind
auspicious as hawks'. Orestes will return soon to find
her terrified of his strong arm and sword. Serpentine, oneiric furies, ophidian
venom are the children you bore for your tragedy, Clytemnestra.
                                   The nightmare
that comes to everyone sooner or later of dying at the hands of their only son.

Two Greeks in the Roman Army

Why do you turn over in bed
away from me, beloved?
Why sleep so late. It's morning.
I regret what I said.

Forgive me. It's a feast day.
What did the augur say?
"Fear time and the dead
who pursue you daily

for the blood you've shed."
We'll sleep in empty
rooms soon enough, our lives
doomed at birth. Rise

from your drunken slumber.
We must march to borders
far from home on orders
from an emperor

whose words are always lies.
Let us be, till then,
not fighting men,
but free, wild as bull, panther

lion, pard, or snake, seditious,
treasonous,
and beautiful as Dionysos
when life's seen at last in all its senseless glory.

Poets of the Late T'ang

for W. S. Milne

May the covers of the book a man is reading build a wall
between him and the vanishing world. May its words
and images keep him free from loss and harm
so that what he finds expressed between its bindings is all

he needs to know to please him. Today, may no birds
fly past his window as premonitions, no alarm
sound to frighten him, no dreadful news relay
more of what he'd early learned about suffering

and pain. Since reading is his favorite way to pray,
let ancient masters recite their poems, say
them aloud to him as he ponders them in his bed,
feeling what their hearts felt, seeing what their keen eyes

observed and knew—poets who'd survived into the clarity of age
like him, white-haired, half-forsaken men, less wise
than wistful as they write still of autumn, still of spring,
of all creation lasting past us, season after season, page after page.

Despair, after Dante

I. Hell

Adulterous lovers, murdered together: who
alive can see them without pitying them, circling,
swirling in a ceaseless storm, bound to
each other in pain and incessant suffering,

their souls tied like ropes into a gordian knot
that's a caricature of lovers embracing when
murdered? To twist in whirlwinds is their lot
now and forever, never to be freed or forgiven.

And for what, for whose fault? Or see Brunetto Latini
rushing as if terrified round a fiery
racetrack, Dante's mentor in poetry,
in Roman history and Cicero. But he was guilty

of loving men, and, though Dante deigns to keep
his company for a few brief moments,
his poem damns him since everyone must reap
what they've sown by a decree that never laments

for the suffering of sinners when in the scheme
of things it is just. Or consider Gianni Schicchi.
reviled, despised by Dante. (The theme
of every encounter in Hell is the same. Eternity

insists that, after death, the doomed soul
be reduced to a trope, not quite imaginary
but a metaphor for someone's whole
life shrunk to his damnable sins.) So Schicchi,

thrust deep in his hell hole, must with his fangs
bite the throat of the half-mad Capocchio,
burned for heresy. Such are the pangs,
the talionic torments, deceivers suffer like a crow

ravaging a susceptible beast yet never satisfying
its hunger. It's true that Dante faints
or weeps before the anguish he is witnessing
at least a few times, listens to some complaints.

But hell is a realm God created for terror, like a sick
man's fantasies of inflicting pain, and Dante,
descending deeper, means to be sadistic,
to taunt, provoke, rage against those, despite their misery,

he hates, despises for his exile, forced wanderings far
from Florence. So Paolo, Francesca, Latini,
Schicchi, all the doomed, are allowed to see no star,
no sun to guide them out of hell, only the infernal sky

everywhere darker than night, though far more stormy.
His descent over, Dante, with Virgil's assistance,
at last reaches the foot of Mount Purgatory
where he will begin his climb to paradise and the dance

it performs to heavenly music. Yet even it depends on cruelty.
Horror, torture, affliction, dread, calamity must exist
for the Law's sake. Since God is Love and Love Justice, agony,
eternal pain must be part of the universal order, must persist

forever in some kind of hell. Though paradise is spared, deaf to the cries
of the punished, listen. Sometimes that moaning, wailing, gnashing
of teeth you hear from Dante's damned souls, are your own sighs
from your despair that there's nothing just about life, no end to its sufferings.

II. *Purgatory*

1.

To dwell for a while in Dante's hell is to remind
yourself of the perilous state of your soul. Whether
before you in the future or far behind
you in the past, hell is everywhere you suffer.

The nature of humanity is maddened by unreason.
I recall a winter chill in the air, dreaded thunder
secluded in clouds. It was at the-end-of-life season:
decay, rot, nothing beautiful, no cause left to wonder

at it. As the morning sun shone on fresh snow,
its shadeless glow invaded my brain,
made my mind freeze. There was nothing to know,
nothing to see, nothing left to gain

by thinking, the world outside too bright
to contemplate, a hell, an icy fire
that turned my thoughts to ashen white,
white as maggots or as the surplices of choir

boys at the altar rail celebrating the host,
devouring the bloody pelt of a woodchuck
festering in woods. I was lost,
a man obsessed with his fate or bad luck.

Snow on more snow. The northern horror
show. Lock the doors. Close the shutters.
Solitude. Turn day to night. I'm a boarder
inside my body's ruined home. My heart flutters

with anxiety, the only god I've ever known.
I'd rather live in an underground cave,
a bony stalactite no lamp ever shone
on by vile spying spelunkers. I hesitate, gravely

quiet as water drips, drips, drips
off me leaving behind its mineral
deposits. As it slowly grows, grips
tighter, the darkness turns funereal.

Without enough fresh air, I can't bear
to breathe, my body cold, my mind
like ice, the despair that's everywhere,
like an underground pool of translucent fish swimming blind.

2.

Stay away, I hear. Go. Leave. Don't knock on Dante's door.
Don't read one more page of his Inferno. It freezes the heart
with its loneliness and suffering, When there's nothing more
to hope for, art can be a monster, scaring you, tearing you apart.

I look up. I see silenced voices, eyeless glances in clouds,
faces long ago faded into a sky the feathery blue
of a jay's spread wings. Dark can't see dark. Ghosts in crowds
are blind to the living around them. It is hard to undo

all that one's done that's untrue. The old grow invisible to others,
become unrecognizable to themselves in memory as in mirrors.
If the body must change, let the soul stay still. Dusk and dawn
reveal the same in-between light, the space between seasons, a mid-storm calm.

When despair leaves the body, who know where it goes? What thrills
the spirit with inspiration if it is not the earth, the clarity
you inherit from light when forgiven? The wind blows softly, chills
me slightly. I want to see it, be as translucent as it is, be in love with reality.

III. *Paradise*

Centuries ago, Thomas Traherne wrote how tears shed
today tomorrow might shine lustrous as pearls.
Night can be a boon if you do not dread
its terrors, the visions it gives you instead, memories of girls

and boys on summer days rushing over hills,
across farms, meadows, or basking in a field
beneath a wide green screen of trees that fills
the horizon with a verdant wall like a massive shield

wielded to spare young eyes from too much light
seen too soon. After years of tears, isn't it worth
falling asleep to glimpse before waking the sight
of the sun's early rising over ivy, vines, and brush

where you and your friends wander at ease as if the earth
has wooed you back to woods where warbler, thrush
and wren perch in trees to sing, like emissaries against despair,
of how bright all things are amidst the sky's magnificence, the dying stars,
the lovely,
       lively air.

History's Forgotten

1.

A red sunset over long shorn southwestern hills.
Clouds dark as cliffs shrouded in shadows.
Night falls from the sky, spills
onto the sea. Waves crash on pinnacles. Crows
soar like bad omens out of the night,
far off shore. Across the Atlantic, a war
waits for its newest recruits to smite
you and so many more.
There's an ocean yet to cross. many miles to go
before you fight across a continent
What will be left for you to know
of peace? Fields of death, towns of sorrow,
your severed life forever spent
in alien soil not many more days after the loss of tomorrow.

2.

The living lie buried with the dead under stones.
A father reads
to his son of Jairus' daughter, led
back to the bible by his need
for a miracle. His wife listens, prays it might end,
the unbearable
dying of a child, envisions
Jesus as a thin, sad man walking beside
a lake where a bird appears
to nest in mid-winter, the season belied
by flowers blossoming at year's
end as her eyes follow
her Lord's passage out of her sight
even while she tugs his hem
and begs him for mercy and weeps
and sorrows

as if he might
yet save her son and keep
him from harm when she's buried
in the graveyard with him
under one stone at the same lonely time of night.

3.

So let us wander, you and me, at our ease in
a meadow in late May
that, by its flourishing, hides all sins.
Thickets of trees. Vines densely
intertwined. Ivy and burr-
bearing brush. See with me
here how time is anonymity
like water,
rocks in a peaceful place, gracefully
shaded by the beauty of green,
kindest of colors.
Though we know unseen
lives lie under earth in a place
like this with no names,
nothing to trace
them by,
the children, men, women,
I mean,
who dwelled here then,
before the war, carefree of a Sunday in a sunny glen
happy, a few even serene
yet ignorant, like us all, of a future
that shames
us before we can know about it or be sure
of what it means to show us of the lives history's forgotten.

What Is History?

1.

Three boys, their father plant cotton in fields a highway
rushes past on the far eastern side. Darnel,
mustard, scrub hedges, hay
stacks edge the rest. A stone wall and well
stand by a shingled barn. It's dawn.
Crows in trees, unfurling their wings,
look like silhouettes sketched or drawn
by a deft hand against the sky. A warm spring's
rains have soaked the loamy, brittle clay.
Pulled by a mule, a plow cuts furrows into the earth.
Sometimes a bone bit or pot shard or parts of a rifle
last shot long ago might be dug up, nothing of worth
or any value, tossed aside, out of the way, like things
from the past not meant to be thought about, whether too good or awful.

The four live in a weathered old farmhouse. Large nests
of wasps or hornets dangle from eaves the spare-
tire faded gray of swings. The clapboard is splintering.
Why have I gone back home, why am I there
on a gravel driveway off the dirt road, sitting
in a car, door open, as if memory suffices to test
what is real or not. Kudzu grasps onto posts.
Weeds choke the porch's bannisters. The humid air
is too hot to breathe. Old men like me wander as ghosts
do, I guess, passing through time's walls. The youngest boy's hair
is shiny as tar yet darkens more whenever he and I swim naked
in the river where it's grown deep as a lake from the downstream
dam that the county had begun and left unfinished, like a dream
you wake up from fearful, as if the living in it felt far less real than the dead.

2.

Now it's a summer day, thistles poking out of clay,
ivy-entwined thickets, magnolia, backwoods in shade

and half-shadows, hawks, blackbirds, a blue jay,
a scrappy feral cat squabbling with crows, the jade-

like pale green of restless leaves and wild grass,
chipmunks, squirrels, hardwood pine, persimmon,
a creek winding to a pond. The man, his boys pass
each other slowly as they work under a blazing sun.

Two lizards slink across a muddy bank, slither
into woods where tree frogs croak among fir
and oak stands. This is how it might have been
in the past, the world peaceful and happy and green,

though in my mind the sun is always a fiery white
that dries the dew-wet fields every morning
even as wild flowers wilt from heat. There's a bite
to the cutting July air, brittle shrubs smelling

of dust, the acrid odor of slate and rock piles,
blistering hot. I listen to the tired drawl
of their voices as they sweat in the heat,
working hard while I hide behind fences or stiles

watching them tend row after row of cotton. Let me call
back to them out of my world as if I could repeat
what happened to me in fantasies, like a lover of histories
who becomes the past he reads of and lives with, yet never truly sees.

3.

Sometimes desires survive much longer
than bodies do. The sun blisters trees,
singes leaves, grass, acorns drop far
too early in the season. August deceives

us with its storms.　Wind-ripped limbs pinging,
ringing on cedar-shake roofs.　Cats,
squirrels scatter bark while climbing
pine trees.　A few thin mice and rats

lie quiet, flattened by the heat.　Dark massed
clouds, stricken by sheet lightning,
turn pale as cotton.　A sudden blast
of stricter winds sweeps up dust, blowing

it in off unseeded fields.　Ripening rows
of corn bend to the rain when it falls,
seem to bow to the thunder until all grows
silent as it passes westward.　One wren calls

to another as the waters flooding
the land quickly recede, the mud
left behind drying quickly, cracking
in zigzag patterns like plates of blood-

red baked clay.　The earth smells sweet
as loam.　Yet that night the sky
felt heavier under the heat
left over from day while he and I

stared out his window at stars flaring,
meteorites crashing, burning
up.　The thick air was throbbing,
pulsing to the beat of our racing

hearts as we waited for nothing, no one,
praying tomorrow's sun
not rise too quickly, not wanting
to forget what we'd just done,

the desire, the fever, swelter, heat
of it pouring out of us, the ache,
the need, the passion we'd repeat
if we could, confess for its own sake,

tell if we could speak of what's impossible
to speak of: how the night air grew
cooler and moths, made visible
by moonlight, wanting out, calmly flew

over us, buzzing in the quiet with no logic
to any of it, we two never able to say
a word about that night or the day
after since all of youth is inexplicable anyway,

inhumanly beautiful, strange, and tragic.

4.

The rain quits at dawn. When birds begin
to sing, we walk to the river,
sit on a boulder, feeling kin
to no one but ourselves. The teeming water
overflows its banks. He grasps
a branch of a pin oak that fell in
during a recent storm, clasps
it tighter as its trunk slides further
into the torrent. Two jays caw
at squirrels shinnying up a pine. Sunlight, fierce and raw,
seeps through clouds. A hound brays at a last sliver
of the moon as he tosses a clay clod in to test the power
of its flow, how far the river might carry us through low
brush banked by forests past farmlands to wherever it wants to go.

II

In Praise of Antonio Vivaldi

for Clarinda Harriss

You can almost hear how Venice's misty light at dawn
softens the basilica's gold to a tawny color
like antique ivory or the coat of a new-born fawn
in a tapestry. Near by, clearly audible, a gondolier's oar
splashes past in the canal as you envision a castrato
wearing a huge white wig and sheeny silk breeches
singing roulades so embellished all sense of the scene
disappears. Our lives are all about mistaken identities,
too: an idyllic romance, a forlorn lover, a father keen
to avenge his son's loss. Forget. Live on. Forgive.
Be magnanimous. So what if the plot makes no sense? Orlando
is mad again. Caio rages. Floria weeps. Titus ponders who will live,
who will die. It is often scary to be trapped in an old libretto
like those Metastasio wrote. But aren't all our life-long dreams
baroque? Each a work of elaborate artifice, no matter how real it seems?
Happenstance and tragedy. Comic interplay. Confusions. Sorrow and joy and wit.
Be glad our lives are imaginary. They make room for paradise. And you and me in it.

Saint Saens' Piano Concerto in C minor

A winding country road still passable avant la guerre
to a melancholy Louis Quinze chateau now American
owned and updated, the lost gardens restored, where
he heard an haute-contre tenor whose voice began
flute-sweet then grew plaintive, grieving like an oboe
as he sang melodies, arias like moonlight on taut silk,
like wisps of mist floating past a half-curtained window
opening toward hills that shadowed a low valley, milk-
white slivers of ice floating on ponds or drifting down stream
toward the river. Offering a silver spoon laid on an ancient gold
plate a venerable waiter served the guests macarons like a dream
of an ancien regime courted by Lully, Leclair, Rameau, lovely, formal,
dance-like, and full of artifice, like the miraculous grace left over in all old
cherished things that cannot be replaced with anything finer or less mortal.

Gabriel Fauré's Piano Quartet in C minor

Mid-summer once shone on us as it gleams in romantic French
music, lustily bright, yet subdued by shade and shadows
that render blunt hues subtler the way, after mornings drench
woods' wild flowers and garden-rich meadows with showers,
they take on the lustrous harmonies and rainbow colors
of cut-glass jars and crystal vials displayed on windowsills: lilies,
salvia, tulips, cowslips, thistles, Lady's slippers,
cinquefoil, peonies, daisies all glowing while marigold and poppies

blushed even redder than the scarlet stains plums from his garden made
on his sun-tanned skin after he had devoured them greedily,
though soon the bruise-like small splotches faded
into a few barely noticeable tiny blushes that in shade
vanished as quickly as the thin, pink scratches I'd left on his body
after we'd made love to Fauré's quartet as it soared and swelled, passionate and florid.

Il Trovatore

The troubadour wanders as if lost in the night,
singing in shadows. His beloved
waits for him to appear when first light
breaks faintly, then intensifies to a flaming red,

its smoldering, ashen smoke dirtying the sky
until it's soot-black as the kettle his mother
cooks in, the stew she swears by,
the vengeance she must ceaselessly stir

in her pot. The enmity between brother and brother
is the only food she needs to survive. "See
how you'll die, who like the sun, enemy
of my darkness, would shine fearlessly as a lover,

who think yourself child of my womb. We live by hatred,
my boy, in one conflagration, one fire, searing and sunset red."

Pirate Jenny

Und wenn dann der Kopf fällt, sag ich: Hoppla!

In Brecht's politics, Weimar is always breaking apart: Jenny's
clutching a shawl round her shoulders,
tapping her foot as she cries
Hoppla!, then turns her mouth down as she savors
the sour banjo evoking memories
of daily despair, bread lines, riots, trillion mark
notes. But it's not just an act or theory, these cruelties.
Jenny is waiting for her freighter to embark

from its port with a skull for its masthead, fifty
cannons, eight sails as it cruises into
the harbor where, see?, she's flinging
her arms up to signal to the pirates its time to start firing,
to burn the town down, kill all its people, annihilate history
so they can sail away like all revolutionaries from all they ever knew.

The New York School

1. Jackson Pollock

Read the obituary pages. Say their names
out loud, guys dead at sixteen, twenty-three,
forty, killed while driving on the plains,
over mountains at the wheel of their Chevy
or modified Ford, having failed to make
the unlit turn on a dark road, crashing
into a lone tree or ice-age boulder, brakes
failing or from a night of riotous drinking
with his buddies, the car's tires still spinning
when a cop throws a flashlight on the wreck.
The joy of risk, of a life sacrificed to speed,
the rush of humanity to return to earth. Painting
is like that, daring death at every turn, every flick
of the wrist, or spontaneous dance of hands and feet,
like a drunk doomed to go beyond where he can see, driving crazily.

2. Mark Rothko

An ancient Jewess sits on a stool, a wicker basket
of trinkets for sale on her lap. It's the Lower
East Side shortly before Shabbat begins. Let
her be. That's all she asks. She's the Lord's daughter.
Her eyes regard the world with the rapt intensity
of someone blinded by a surfeit of vision, by its greater
illumination. She's feeding pigeons with bits of cheese. See
what she observes as they perch on wires or rooftops,
swoop down, fly back with food in their beaks while she empties
her eyes. The sun is slowly diying behind the crowded row
of tenements. It is the holy time. She walks inside hers, stops
all her labors. A tragic luminosity is shining from the last glow
of sunset over the city even as the moon rises, almost invisibly,
over a line of high rises as streetlights start to glare The old woman sees none
of this in her unlit room, all shades drawn, shorn of icons, as the Lord's ordered done.

32

3. *Ad Reinhardt*

Years ago, at a museum's juried show, Ad Reinhardt made
his picks with precise black marks, choosing only paintings
as black as his own, abstractions that forbade
all attempts to find meanings in them, just things
silently hanging on gallery walls, delineated geometries,
perceived as squares only if stared at carefully,
not revelations but dark gradations of subtleties,
their hints of color saying only there's nothing to see
but art for art's sake: that is, if anyone really knows
what art is save for a not quite absolutely black painting's
obscure, slight manifestations of the fact that what it shows
means nothing at all, for what is Nothing if not a nearly blank thing
backed by a blanker white wall? So, you see, there's a kind of purity
to it, isn't there?, as if someone is trying to say, "My friends, listen. I'll miss
only this by dying: art's ironic beauty, the stark dark fact of its utter uselessness."

4. *Willem de Kooning*

Walking alone through the Village during a fierce
blizzard, listening to the sibilant sighs snow makes
falling on the city as it quiets his lingering fears
about his old world ways, thrilled by how its flakes
sweep over Manhattan until in his eyes the island disappears–
streetlights, taxis, tenements, brownstones,
bars, cinemas all abstracted by the storm. A tug nears
the harbor, people struggle off, its horns' moans
muffled by howling winds. Radio static seeps
through a transom. He hears bits of jazz, recalls,
for no reason, the old masters, the paintings he keeps
trying to forget, seeking the freedom to see in random walls
layered with posters and ads and graffiti the same glimpse
of reality he's discovering in a city half-hidden by snow. A dog limps
past him in the slush. The light is baffling, the city nearly transparent
in the snow, radiant as the melting ice flowing from a laundry's steaming vent.

From a Letter Addressed by a Young Poet to André Breton

Only a few remnants of the old village are still
standing. A sandier, more friable soil covers
the dark dense earth far below. The river spills
detritus from the flood into the sea, its water
no longer potable. Sisters walk hand in hand
only where they're permitted to go, brothers
barter clothes for food. It's an unhappy land
they live in. No more fathers. No more mothers.
Last week, a wild child was found skulking in
the public garden, sticks and weeds infested
with pests. The sky blackens. The air thickens.
Rats seek holes to hide in from the sun. The dead
are said to speak. At night, ghosts glide over
the steaming lake like mist rising out of roiling water.

Holidays, naked revelers snake through a crowd
of gawking children whose rage is masked as
laughter. Smoky clouds, fiery sunsets enshroud
the sky. The moon is a sliver of golden topaz
encased in a ring of silver. A boy lies in bed,
claws pawing at him in the dark, making
him sweat. He dries himself with a rag, treads
lightly on the floor, trying to be quiet, not waking
the others. He smells leaking gas and the stink
of rotting flesh as night workers lay out bodies
on the beach. Try not to dream, not to think
of the world anymore except as a surrealist sonnet
that makes sense of nothing but our mad fantasies
of dying since, he says to André, "J'ai une allergie à la planète."

A Last Recital

1.

During her farewell tour, at her last recital
at Zellerbach, following encore after encore,
Elisabeth Schwarzkopf, in the darkened hall,
lowered the keyboard's cover and left. There'd be no more.

Years before, when asked what one thing most
characterized her art, she answered, "Longing.
Nostalgia." It was the heart of her singing, that lost
world some place that never was, silently waiting

for us all. After great age had ravaged her beauty,
she refused to be photographed, but did not discard
her old pictures, her speaking voice still distinctly
hers, like an exile's looking back, sadly glancing homeward.

2.

Nostoi. Nostalgia is the beginning and end of art.
Penelope sits by her loom, crippled by age,
unable to weave, an erratic beat to her heart,
her fingers arthritic. Odysseus has journeyed to a savage

land far away where he can plant an oar in desert sand
and declare at last at end to his voyaging, never
to return to her. She says silently, "Dear husband,
come home." But what is she wishing for? For some endeavor

to be more real than the world they'd lost? Yet none
of her tapestries survived her artistry, the sense
of them in their having been each night unraveled, undone,
as if art meant nothing more than life's coming hither, then going hence.

Why Write?

The fog is like gray chiffon billowing in the wind,
a wide scrim hiding the horizon it obscures behind
the mist. Two hungry hawks circle above it, climb
higher, then perch on a branch of a Bishop pine.
A precipice. Serrated, bluff cliffs. Boulders,
fallen rocks battered by encroaching waters.
Pelicans appear out of western clouds, fly
back into the shroud where invisible gulls cry.
By the gate to the bay, foghorns moan
deep as Russian basses chant their ritual drone.
Playful seals, otters, a surfer riding waves alone,
a jam jar tossed intact on the beach, driftwood,
a drenched scarlet scarf, a polished, iridescent stone.
What is there to say if none of this can be understood?

The world is changing. A woman closes her shutters against
a chill wind. Far off, crab boats simulate small islands.
The ocean stays calm, though pelicans, having sensed
the shift in season, fly as a flock over drifting sands.
In the park, a man walks through brush into a pathless
thicket hazy as a rainforest's. Migratory birds
rest by a lake that raccoons slip into. A sticky mess
of algae clings to their soaked fur. Mere images, words.
An early sun is testing itself against the fog, a radiant
dawn attempting once more to fill the sky over hill country
and the bay below. There is so much to forget, to recant
about a life that the end of it leaves us bewildered, with scant
consolation. What is there to say? As fog and light, sky and sea
flow into each other, when everything's nebulous, nothing's clear, it's time to be
silent.

Misreadings

I dreamed I was translating a German Romantic poem
about edelweiss and roses, babbling brooks,
stone wells, a hearth fire in a thatch roof home,
hay reapers, milk maids, old shepherds with crooks

watching sheep in meadows, panting dogs, a nesting wren,
a soaring jay, Anna's newfound love for Erik,
his for her in a world, the poem said, "keine klagen,"
without pains or griefs or sorrows, pastoral and poetic.

Yet, as morning broke, the poet, who had died young
of consumption, rose out of my sleep to complain.
"You're reading an editor's corrupt version. It's wrong.
'Kleine,' not 'keine'. My poem is a little lament, a song

that's sad no matter how happy it seems to be, like rain
falling in sunshine, flowering meadows, ripening grain,
while a boy, tilling a field, coughs up spots of blood
on a handkerchief he mistakes for specks of wet red mud."

III

The Earth Floats in Water, after Thales

After a clear night, the fog settles back in, thick as in a movie
I'd seen that was set in wartime London, spies plotting,
the Thames their getaway, saboteurs showing no pity,
secret agents assassinating MPs. Even the mist, growing
heavier and denser, was as guilty of subterfuge
as the enemy's scheming, conniving to subvert the vision
of a humanity who in the film seemed to merge
into the foggy, blurred dawns they woke to. London
was hazy, obscure anyway from fires still smoldering
and smoking after night after night of bombings, rumors
of invasion spreading, whether by land or by the river,
while the police were barely able to do their jobs, trying
to help the men, women, children seeking refuge in the under-
ground where they waited, wondering, warily looking at one another,
afraid of fog, smoke, bombs, of the world above unbreathable, drowned in water.

It's hard to see past the Great Highway
to the dunes only a few yards away. A shroud
conceals the lowlands. If you plan to pray,
pray now, I guess, before a massive cloud
blinds the city and its hills. Someone
is banging on a trash can. A Monterey
pine is bent by winds that are cracking its
limbs. Someone is shouting, sounding afraid.
A car backfires. A child cries. A restless ocean
surges and recedes over and over. The blitz
was like that in the movie: an hours long raid
on a clear night, then the fog returning as in San
Francisco it always does after sunset. What did Thales
mean by saying Reality is One and the One, the Absolute, is water?
That everything that rises must converge to float and drown like the earth in its seas?

41

Woodland Legend

In a North Carolina old growth forest, far back
into it, a mystery: how noon's full
light falls through trees to show each track
left by wild animals in dirt and duff as if the woods pull

sunlight deeper down upon dripping ferns, damp stones,
small furry or feathered creatures scurrying across
needle-, leaf-strewn ground or over bones
glistening like wet polished limestone pocked with moss.

Here is the mythic sun-lit realm of arboreal ashes,
cliff face rubble, dead limbs, twigs after catastrophes,
the wind storm, hurricane, or tempest that crashes
through the shaken forest to harm what it pleases,

uprooting feeble old trees, eroding frail limestone
cliffs crumbled, slivered by ceaseless cascades.
Stand naked in a cool, winding creek alone
and feel exalted by winds blowing over sunny glades,

through vivid marshlands. There's a minatory shade-
less glare in woods by late summer, the course
of your life unknown, yet showing you the way to what made
light fall so intently on this primeval place, revealing its heavenly source.

Waterfall

for Nathan Wirth

Yes, in an old growth forest, what is most beautiful is not fact
exactly, but a mystery unexplained by noon's full
light. Fungus-whitened bark, rotted limbs, cracked
boulders, shadowy canopies: each seems to lull
the woods out of its deep sleep, ferns, dripping stones,
trickling creeks from night's runoff streaming across
needle-, leaf-strewn humus, furless pelts, black bones
lying only half buried by leaves, twigs, green shrouds of moss.
A man wades in a cool brook on slippery sandstone
as a cascade pounds on him like waves breaking so fiercely
on his back he feels exalted by what surely must be the truth,
the real thing he's been given by the undimmed presence of the forest
at noon where all the universe seems to have converged to test
itself in the raging power of the falls that originates far away in its distant youth,
in its origins high up in the mountains, much too remote for him to climb there to see.

Feeding Birds

It is a rainy day mingled with sleet without any breaks
between storms, a day more suitable to Lent
than December's holidays. The roads are lakes,
the gutters icy streams. Is this what his life has meant?
An old man, a phantom, sits alone in a doorway
garbed in mourning, disheveled, gaunt, and pensive.
From a large paper sack, he's tossing food to wet gray
pigeons and drenched starlings. The birds look apprehensive,
perched on dangling tree limbs or roofs. They swoop down
from time to time to peck at seeds, then swiftly fly
back, their beaks spilling shells as they eat. The crown
of a cardinal droops like the man's floppy soaked cap. The sky
says more bad weather is on the way. He knows he must die
soon. The man is my good friend and this is the last clear memory
I have of him. Inside, he closes all the curtains until there's nothing left to see.

A Grove of Willows by the Side of a River in a Storm

I'm a boy freed by woods where the plague can't find
him as he floats in a lake or sprawls by it waiting
for the sun to warm its cool, spring-fed water.

Ronnie's peeing into bushes while hiding behind
a tree. I feel as if I'm safe, as if I've nothing
to be afraid of, rejoicing in the tangy smell of the fir.

I believe God is everywhere. I believe the earth is good
and summer will last forever. It is easy to rest
here, to bask on the soft grass and moss along the shore.

Ronnie lays his head on my chest. So little is understood
about love. In late life it's like returning to the forest
where I first knew what it felt like, never to ask for more.

The jays are cawing, robins singing, wrens, swallows
perching on branches or twigs. I can hear Ron sigh
soft as the morning breeze before we both fall back to sleep.

Suppose it is this peaceful, whatever it is that follows
existence, a lake waiting at your feet, a forest in July,
two boys waking, wading into it to explore how cold it is, how deep.

The Garden of Love

1.

Making love with you was like entering through the gate
of a secret garden, using the key you gave me
to meet you by salvia and rose beds where you'd wait
for me in the morning, you'd said, after the sun slowly

had risen over the tree-lined horizon, warming the chill,
dew-wet air night leaves behind it even after dawn
and the sun tops the tallest walls' shadows, the day still
and quiet for a while as if hopeful, or afraid?, of being drawn

by light's strength out of time into a place like the edenic
promise of a world elsewhere, the sun climbing ever
higher, hotter in a sky blindingly bright and, like music
played too glaringly almost deafening yet also clear,

glorious, too, excessive, yes, romantic as the garden itself,
not formal but free to grow, flourish on its
own, left alone, like a wilderness whose florid wealth
belongs to no one, to nothing, and so never quits

thriving and never seems not to mind those few who
trespass in it so long as they keep its secret
like that of the garden whose key you gave me to
breach its gates, permitting me to lie with you in it as if to let

me know what gifts a body wants to give, what generosity,
clarity it offers, one to the other, the metaphysical moment
when flesh and soul unite in pleasure, ecstasy,
the sun shining on a garden so fully awakened every taste, scent,

sound, sight, touch of it is intensified into the reality
of a love, a passion recollected even many years after
by a memory that embraces us in its favored, romantic imagery,
where we rest on its soft damp grass again, drink from its creek's sweet water.

2.

Green things dreaming of two young men,
of new leaves sparkling,
winged seeds drifting
across a garden,

white, silvery threads of dandelion
shimming at dawn
turning golden
when sun-lit,

floating in light as if it were air,
the alchemical
miracle,
the secret remit

of a philosopher's stone,
transforming
base metal into gold,
body to soul, how it does so unknown,

still a mystery to us now we're old,
reminiscing
about salvia, wild roses,
blue flag irises,

tiger lilies, the garden we,
our bodies
were, what we'd sown
there,

an electric charge to the air,
some trick
of heat
it knew how to keep

like the secret between us
as we sipped
from a creek
seeing ourselves mirrored

by its cool, well-like water
brothers, lovers
drowning in each other's
sun-lit, shining, sweating naked bodies

like Narcissus at his pool.

An Emperor's Garden

Like you as you spy at him, the emperor of Zhou
wanders in the Park of the Spirit.
Deer kneel on grass to feed their fawns.
The feathers of cranes as they fly by
are thrice adored in morning's splendor.
He strolls beside the Lake of the Soul
that its waters might nourish him. Golden
fish feed on sunlight that pierces what darkness

persists in a magnolia tree grove near noon,
its blossoms bronze-lipped. Gardenias spice
the air. A row of boxwood. Stickseed burs
clinging to his royal clothes. You hear children
laughing near a stone well at the heart
of a hedge labyrinth. A slow creek overflows
its fern-covered, sloping banks. The sky is paper
white. Stones bask in the silken heat. You say, All is well.

Will o wisp rising. Dogwood blossoming.
Hip-high hedges bordering neighboring woods.
Shadows striding prouder after dawn.
Lazy snakes sinuous as waves in a sinuous
river. A monk strikes a temple bell. Flourishing
flowers grace prayers with scents of spring.
In the lower left hand corner, a sage's robes
are painted bright green, fulgent as the green

of trees aspiring to light, of pine needles pungent
as incense. You see? Beauty, sensuality is what
the screen means by paradise: how a world that never was
is to be forever remembered. Sun, sun again shining
on petals falling slowly to please the prince of earth
and heaven wherever he walks, like the cone-shaped
mist-masked hills loosely inscribed in the hazy background
you keep bowing to long after you depart Wen Wang's fabled guarded garden.

Veneration

He is an old man listening to a dying tree tell him its story for the last
time, an ancient oak with noble roots alone in a stand
of maple and pine sap-quickened by sunshine under a vast
sky that gratefully pours its light on a burgeoning land
as if it were a kind of paradise composed only of things
of the earth and nothing more, rippling streams, honey bees
sipping from flowers blossoming after mid-spring
morning showers, wind-tossed petals, ferns unfurling, turtles
basking on rocks, birds singing whatever it pleases
them to sing, snakes awakened by sunlight, skittish squirrels
playing their comic parts in the romance between green boughs.
and spring as the man breathes in the cool, sweet air redolent
with the scents of May one last time, for the hour has come for him to drowse,
to sleep, lying like a lover beside his beloved oak beneath a widening firmament,
listening to it speak as it shakes its limbs in the wind and sighs and drops its rusty
leaves.

Mojave

His father demands Ishmael be driven out,
exiled into the empty quarter of Arabia
where his mother dies of thirst, the sun
dizzying, like Hagar feverish, and she with nowhere to lay
her head safely as her child aimlessly wanders about
the vast, barren
desert while the scirocco's raw,
blistering winds in a skin-piercing sand storm burn
his mind into a vision of desolation
more blinding than the angels Abraham said he saw.

In the Mojave, the summer air is febrile, unbreathable.
Why did you dare me to go there?   To see
what? The brittle skeletal bits of creatures scattered in dried
arroyos? Or to hear in the heat how emptiness speaks, sputtering and parched?

A Beachside Liturgy

It is a dingy day, the clouds the colors of slightly
singed paper, white and gray blotched by black
spots and streaks. The surf's been stirred up by
storms just beginning far south. All the Pacific lacks
now is fury and rage. Yet lots of surfers, always intrepid,
dare the waves anyway. An animal, though not
a seal or otter this time but a big dog, lies dead,
sprawled out on the beach as if left to rot.
Its fur is the yellow of dry sand, its thick, long
tail the burnt-sugar brown of the wet patches
around it. Another large dog waits a hundred feet
or so off, contemplative, mournful as a Nile sphinx.
A couple stands watch, clearly unwilling to let the sea's
rising waves seize the body for its own at high tide. What is meet
and right is to praise each life lost no matter what one thinks
or believes about souls. So they hum to it a newly made-up wordless song.

IV

Unheimlichkeit

Late night under the rusty glow of streetlights, a dim
moon. Fogged-in gray Victorians. Sooty warehouses,
their plate glass windows cracked or broken, grim
to look at like a sort of bitter warning that seizes
the abandoned soul. Boots click-clack, click-clack
like tap shoes on the pavement. Ruts in cement
trap and squeeze pockets of weeds. Painted black,
a picket fence lines a block-sized excavation. The scent
of damp piles of sand and dirt seeps out of the pit. Rest
here awhile in your dream of the life you thought
you'd escaped. The sound of nails on worn shoes, like a test
of forbearance, pounds on. But no one is there. You're alone.
And can't wake up even as you hear someone cry, "You ought
to go home now. It's time." Out of the dark city comes that plea, that admonition.

The House on Telegraph Hill

At the foot of Telegraph Hill, on every side
save the west, lie piles of rocks, massive
stones, boulders, the proof no one can hide
of what has slid, fallen or been forced (elusive

as evidence is) off its cliffs for centuries after
erosive storms. In one story, a man was said
to shove his wife through a hole he'd made bigger
in a shed floor that dangled over a ledge she'd

stood by with him safely before. The tale is woven,
tangled with threads of false love and greed
made knottier, impossible to untie or to loosen
by forgotten histories, lost documents—what you'd need

to know to ascertain truth, especially about a boy's
considerable inheritance if his beloved mother
died. But the past is easily confused with decoys
of it, facsimiles, fabrications, lies of one sort or another

that mimic reality. And yet listen to Telegraph Hill's
green parrots' chatter as they eat nuts and berries.
You might find in the birds a beauty that fills
you with wonder and frees you from useless worries.

But suppose you also detect in their voices the earth's
solidity cracking as a woman plummets off a precipice
crying wildly at the shock of her descent, how her death's
befallen her like the collapse of the rational, betrayed by a kiss.

A Childhood Romance

for Tommy Gold

1.

Summer-seared leaves
were rustling
in the breeze
as the moon woke
us. We
stared out the window
eager to see, to look

at how, like crushed oil on asphalt, red, gold, blue
rings haloed stars. Slug slime trails
on a sill, a black beetle inching

up a screen, the rattle of bamboo
against a wall, a fence's rails
ringing from a tree branch's beating

against it: nothing new about it but how real it felt to be with you.

2.

After a day spent under a Carolina sun,
twilight descends
suddenly upon
us, darkening woods

and every watchful tree as, one
by one, each pretends
to have begun
to sleep at night like us. What good

is hope for eternal
life if a river,
a bridge's signal

lights for boats to pass under
it, are all we can see
outside our window, flickering and flowing.

3.

A Sunday sky's the faded
blue and white
of hand-painted
porcelain. A solemn early light

shimmers to the sounds
of church bells'
reverberations. The ground's
been sweetened by rain. A spell's

upon us, like that of sages in a scroll
you showed me,
old masters of gardens

who believed each flower has a soul,
you said, maybe
to tease me, a spirit wiser than men's.

4.

A buzzing housefly, a green lynx spider,
a slumbering cat, ripe peaches on a plate,
a sky the pure blue of the water
where later we'll float two paper boats downstream,

a porch where your father's homemade cider
waits for us in a glass pitcher,
our lying side by side on grass by the gate
to the road, a barking wild dog: no theme

unites a life into only one meaning, not even the sun
shining upon the toy boats we'd made
to watch drift further and further from home

weightless as feathers or petals, both of us ready to abandon
them as they sail away, as if we, too, had strayed
from where we had started, longing to wander, to be free to roam.

5.

The white, sticky, cottony threads
the dandelion
by the pond sheds
the same time each year is falling lightly on

grass and scattered patches of mud. Winged seeds
from trees flitter past
us as kudzu, ivy, weeds
seem to tighten their grips on things. What will last

among these flowers and leaves,
sparkling, rippling
in the wind like a lake in morning light?

We steal each other's hearts like thieves,
I suppose, not meaning to, waking
naked in bed together, gripping each other, holding on tight.

6.

This evening, no wind blows over fields from river
to river. How does it begin,
the grip of winter
on children?

The dying sun is tarnished, a yellow, flat, cold
disc that refuses to move
as clouds hold
onto it secretly like a king a treasure trove

he intends to show off later. No birds sing
in their perches.
No squirrel or chipmunk searches

for nuts or seeds. It's a scene of desolation
I'm remembering:
two logs trapped in a dark lake, frozen, abandoned.

7.

Plush grass, trellised vines, white lattice
work that encloses
a stone well
at the heart of an imaginary garden,

begonia, camellia, clematis,
cinquefoil, roses.
I want to tell
you about all I've forgotten,

to remind you how I stood beside you
as we tried to stare
into the deepening traces

of a well too dark deep down to see through
to the bottom, to dare
it to reveal the secrets it hid, reflected off our faces.

8.

Two boys are dripping their thick milky seed
onto a brown rag rug, white as sails
on sailboats, as crests of waves.
There is nothing to plead
guilty to, is there?, we agree. Nothing fails
us this morning. True passion saves
no one from dying young, but at dawn the dew
on wet stones sparkles gladly, the ground
glitters in early morning light while hosts of locusts
drone in weeds, by trees with their mating sound,
buzzing and hissing and roaring all night. I love you.
Dawn adores you. If nature knows more than we do about lust's
ways with us, the morning after breathes easily, deeper at first
light. What is this thing we are, this abiding need, this hunger, this thirst?

9.

Nothing can redeem
the past.
It simply lasts
for the sake
of paradise, two boys in ecstasy.
The lake
flows over the dam into the stream
below, its banks a garden
of ferns and wild grasses for teenage boys
like Tommy and me
to lie on,
in fantasy,
in desire ever unsatisfied,
always to be grasped for, beyond mortality.

A Childhood Romance, Again

1.

When will happiness return
from wandering
with its journeyman's sack
on its back
with nothing left to learn
from living?

Summer-seared leaves
drop into a brook
translucent
as the moon
you woke me to. What grieves
me most is the look
on your face as if I'd meant
to hurt you with all I'd confessed too soon.

2.

After a day of Georgia sun,
twilight descends
suddenly upon us,
shading woods.

Every watchful tree, one
by one, rends
our treasonous
souls apart. What good

is the love of maternal
night for the river,
the bridge's signal

lights as boats pass under
it, if we are not taken
by darkness into its arms and forgiven?

3.

The Sunday sky's the faded
blue and white
of antique hand-painted
porcelain. A happy light

shimmers to the sounds
of church bells'
reverberations. The ground's
been sweetened by rain. A spell's

upon us, like images of a scroll
of sages, late
masters of gardens,

joking, laughing about the toll
life takes upon those who wait
too long to grieve and be cleansed.

4.

A housefly, a green lynx spider,
milkweed, peach pits, a sky
the crystalline blue of the water
where our paper boats float downstream

On the porch, your father's hard cider
waits for us in a tall glass pitcher.
Ferns, soft grass to lie
on. The warm, hospitable gleam

of first light shines invitingly upon
us and the boats we made
as we watch them sailing far from home

soft as petals or feathers, glistening in the sun,
then slowly drifting away, as if played
with too often, ready to sink into a swirling mass of foam.

5.

White silvery threads
of dandelion
spread
thin and sticky as cotton on

wet trees and flowers. Winged seeds
drift past
us. Grass, vines, weeds.
Nothing will last

of us. Spring's new leaves
though sparkling
in dawn's kind light,

like thieves
of the heart, are grieving, too,
as green things do, for all they'd believed was true.

6.

No breezes or winds blow across fields from river
to river. How does it begin,
the hold of December
on children?

The sun is a tarnished yellow flat
disc that seems not to move
in that sky. How explain that?
Or the treasure trove

of light it appears to be? No birds sing
in their perches.
No squirrel searches

for nuts or seeds.   It's a scene of apprehension,
I'm remembering,
the river iced over, the dying sun.

7.

To write on water, in air,
to watch each leaf
disappear,
like all the things you care

for, to despair for lack of belief
in anything's lasting,
to fear
life too much to dare

it: how bear it then, the cry
each time you sleep
you hear and choose

to think a nightmare. "Goodbye.
I did not want to lose
you.   But so I did. And so I weep."

8.

Plush grass, trellised vines, white lattice
work that encloses
a stone well
at the heart of a garden,

begonia, camellia, clematis,
cinquefoil, roses:
you with so much to tell
me of what I've forgotten,

show me again how I stood beside you
as we stared
down into the watery traces

of a well too deep to see all the way through
to the bottom, though it reflected
us as if we'd been one sharing one wish, wearing two faces.

His Cold Companion

1.

Elusive nights, days, the half-lit shadows of dusk
falling, or mornings just beginning,
birds aloft in the light, the rush
of cars on the highway, people crowding

sidewalks, buses, hurrying to work, the sight
of them moving, ever changing, their dreams
over, abandoned to day's fantasies of flight,
perhaps, or a life that's more real than it seems.

It is low tide. The sand has been washed to the color
of reaped hay. Shallow pools lie scattered along
the shoreline where gulls float in quiet water.
Fog mutes the cawing of ravens, a wren's song.

Wearing waders, elderly fisherman cast in the surf.
When the fish is too small to keep, they toss it back in.
In his wetsuit, a surfer wonders if the ride's worth
it on a sea slick and still as snow. The ghost-white sun's moon's twin.

Far away, in a house near a meadow, a man watches a blizzard
confound day. The snow is covering the world in white.
As the moon declines, it is pale as his beloved's face
in a window. The world appears clearer everywhere, unmarred,

while he listens, as if it's a Chopin nocturne, to the play of light
on snow, pale as the moon and stars as they fade with grace.
Yet nothing is ever clear. It is like what he imagines paradise
to be, cold, strange, obscure as the world is, and it alone all he ever sees.

2.

Study a page of philosophical negations, a nocturnal,
metaphysical rumination on oblivion, the all
of self-contradiction,
the dying call

of failing light, the undoing of life by the presentiments
said to belong only to gods, the holy ones
of the not yet, the absent
sons

of tyrannical fathers, the heretofore of unknowing
surging like a mob loosed to riot,
its violence subduing
the Not

of consciousness. Then look up. Observe an old man walking
under storm clouds in cold weather praying
he might live the same wintry life forever,
over and over.

3.

A bird lands on the old man's windowsill, beating its wings,
frantic to get in. It is winter, the first day
of real snow. The cold stings his face. The bird
is thin. It should have flown south but somehow
forgot to. He cannot change its fate to save
it, the bird he spied that morning with the strange,
fast fluttering of its heart, its claws clutching
at nothing. It is always like that when one flies
back to him. He reaches out to feel the air beaten
by its wings while snow flakes, thick and fat, fall
amid distant cracks of thunder breaching the sky.
It is a well-known sorrow that snow wakes him to:
a famished, wet bird pecking at an icy pane he knows
he cannot rescue, no more than those he loves, from the chill in his heart.

4.

A heavier snow has covered the earth in a white
shadowed by trees and tall dolomite
buildings, cold and bare as the moon,
faint as a face peering through a window.
The sky is lucid, a few clouds, soon
to vanish, lingering. There's no sorrow
here, nothing to regret, a morning
lovely as the Schubert being played far away,
barely audible, lyric and gentle, from long ago,
like the voice of someone you know returning
from a distant place you're sure to follow
him back to. So much has been covered by snow
it is hard to find the lost things obscured deep below
it: an oft-read book, a torn scarf, faded letters, a wedding ring.

5.

The elderly hear in the air nothing foreign, nothing
foreboding, just night music lulling them
to sleep as they listen to it sing,
consoling as a hymn.

Their eyes, their half-shut, bright, lovely
eyes, as lovers will do,
seek in the other's face, secretly,
for signs of rescue.

From the peak of a snowy mountain overlooking
the city, the world is gray as the wintery rain
falling daily on everything,
silent as the pain

of waiting for death to refute the brute, blunt lie
that it is the mother of beauty.

6.

Four spindly trees–images from a grove, a stark stand
of charred pine, sewn into blue wool squares
of a quilt–form a pine quaternity with a band
of linen stars around it stitched in pairs.
At its center, black-feathered arrows
are displayed in a golden quiver. Like birds, these trees
are winged. Asymmetries of flowers, plows'
zigzag tracks, decorate the edges. Betrayed geometries
torn from worn cloth patches are what poetry
is made from, the wonders of the undesigned,
miracles found by chance in everything, a solitary
smoldering pine grove, a jonquil, a feather an artist finds
on a walk, signs of past lives too fine to be accidental. Clarity,
perhaps, is like that, like a long, sleepless, frosty night when you see
reality clearer by moonlight's shadows, hear it battering shutters in the crosswinds.

7.

It is just before sunrise. No birds are singing
yet. It is warm for December. Last night's fog
slowly retreats to the mountains. Everything
he sees looks more doubtful in shadowy half light.

A ruined woman sits on the bench of a picnic
table, sobbing into her hands.
She's obviously sat there all night. Some trick
of life has abandoned her here, far

from any home. It can't matter what her name
is. It can't matter if she's sick
or mad. She and he are the same
in a way, cast out from youth and alone.

Nearly all his life he's lived in a lucid place,
working in solitude, observing the habits
of men and women. Her black hair is sand-
gritty, muddy like one acquainted with fits

of despair. Perhaps she has lived a miserable life.
The woman on the bench weeps and weeps.
As he walks closer to her, he thinks of friends
he'd never done enough for, the grief and strife

he'd caused them sometimes. Love should be plain,
simple as the everyday. But, if compassion means
anything, why does she out of the depth of her pain
bang on the table, stare up, and rage, "Useless, it's useless?"

And he, unable to help, say anything to comfort
her, offers her mere money, a few
dollars. What would he do if he knew
who she was: himself on the first ring of purgatory?

Nightfall

As the sky grows darker, bleaker, plaits of light blue,
like tattered swatches from a faded tapestry,
cease shining between clouds but close as curtains do,

obscuring the outside world when playtime is over. Westerly
red and yellow streaks mark the empty horizon. It is dusk,
though a field of wild sunflowers, as if praying

to it, still bows toward sunset. A child is playing with a tusk
he has broken off a porcelain elephant beloved by
his sister as he listens to the porch swing creaking

in the wind. It will be raining hard soon. A large snail
slips through weeds near where he kneels, leaving a trail
of glistening snail-slick behind it. "A boy who's afraid

of thunder and lightning will foolishly cower before any wolf at
his door," his father used to admonish him, upbraid
him for his cowardice. And he is soft. He is fearful. He is frail.

Safer on the porch, the boy fondles the wounded elephant, pets his cat,
waits for night, for the monsters he dreads to stand over his bed,
like Mary Shelley's, pieced back together with lightning and wire and thread.

It's almost fully dark. A feral cat is devouring a tiger-striped butterfly
in the garden. Could green things, thriving flowers offer solace
to his solitude? Maple trees' seedling wings, twisting, speed by,

their veins rusty white and silvery, twirling and twirling, thin as lace.
In an old craggy oak, two jays berate him. He wonders why
they dislike him as he picks off the stickseed burrs clinging to his pants. Ruby

lipped rose petals float in a rippling puddle. A breeze brushes his face,
light as his mother's kisses when she comes to his bed every
time he wakes himself by crying out. He wishes he did not have to be

who is. Fireflies and moths swarm by the screen, batter the door as the rain
intensifies. It is nightfall, only nightfall, I would say to him. Your pain
will end in sleep soon. I am the you you will grow into. Let me tell you our story.

Out in the Dark

The predictions were all wrong. The storm they'd feared
was more savage than they'd said, the flood that followed
eroding the land, destroying all that had endeared
it to its people, wherever it had risen left hollowed
out like dried up river beds in a world changed to deserts.
A school boy hangs his helmet up in a locker. Another
kid, jutting his chin into the wind, stands on a corner
waiting for a bus. How can they know how love hurts?
Yet, hours later, they'll disappear somewhere out of sight
into a forest or a faraway city where it's always midnight
and no one can find them in the dark or pursue or chase after
them since they'll leave no sign behind them. The rising water
cracks windows like breaking ice and flows raging, storm-driven,
and free towards the sea it feeds while two boys lie in bed together,
thrilling to the beauty of its promise. To be wild as a river. And never afraid again.

Civilization

For Susan and Sam Crowl

I. *Nature*

1.

The earth steams. The sky stays misty. A gray cloud rumbles.
Pick berry sprigs for warmer weather. Cicada chirr, flies
and bees buzz, tree frogs croak, throb. Fear no more troubles
this day. Morning begins anew as birds, twittering, spin melodies
to celebrate spring, how even if it rains the day remains lovely.
Woods, a house, choose which will protect you better when
a thunderstorm rages through again. Yet be content, happy
wherever you might find a roof in wilderness or cities. Children,
women, men may be simultaneously innocent and guilty. Joy and terror
rarely dwell far apart. But here forsythia, butterfly bushes, a shade tree
grow by wild roses that cling to fences. Bees carefully sip each flower.
Blackbirds rest on dewy grass. Three cardinals clutch a pine limb as pollen,
swirling like dust, glitters in the air. A hound brays at a waning moon's silver
light as birds flap their wings, squirrels rush through brush on a day as old as this one.

2.

Peach, apple blossoms once fell into your lap. Remember that?
You shook them off, stood up. A stray dog, maybe
feral, rustled through bushes chasing a hissing cat,
barking at a possum. The rain quit at dawn. You roamed easily.
listening to the birds as they resumed their chirruping
and chattering while you sat on a boulder watching
a river exceeding its banks having paused to ponder
why a child easily accepts that steadily flowing water
is a mystery to wonder at, not probe, like change or transience.
You grabbed the strong, thick branch of a sycamore that toppled over
during a recent storm, climbed on its moss-covered trunk

while the sun glared through low, thinning clouds. Maybe, sometimes, loss, absence
might shine like what you saw below the stream, chunks of granite or quartz sunk
in a storm sparkling in the light piercing through its dim depths to the bed of the
river.

3.

Old age might be so beyond understanding that those who write
about it can express it only in parables like this: as crows perform
their dances on a circular, barren patch of ground at night,
in woods deepened by darkness and the violent storm
that's on its way, as pitch-black ravens imitate a hummingbird's
grace while they beat their wings invisibly fast, moving clockwise
in a perfect, choreographed circle, with nothing at all absurd
about them so boldly do they sway to and fro in the guise
of those fluent, elegant, beautiful birds they envy so, as they
silence their clacking beaks and sawing cawing sorrows, clever
at staying quiet, needing only the wind for music, these crows,
I say, these ungainly creatures, proudly strut as if woods were theirs forever,
never aware of, never seeing the child who, though forbidden to, fearlessly goes
into the forest to learn how black-as-night crows are freed by darkness to dance
and play.

II. Memory

Each person now alive may mirror someone who has died
or is yet to be born. Walking through a museum,
you might find a portrait, among those that have survived
time, of a face so familiar it is as if you had known them
all your life, like an actor in a film or in the theater
that resembles a dear friend, a cherished local
person you enjoy talking to, an acquaintance you remember
from your long ago past. All snapshots inevitably plagiarize,
and every photo taken exposes a ghost. 'Now' and 'Then' each doubles
for the other. And the future as likely might discover the bodies

it desires waiting to meet them in faded images of you and yours
left behind in scrapbooks. Every tale told repeats itself. Every word relies
on memory to be written at all. And each dream a dreamer has dreamed recurs
in you who listen to them as if to your childhood's mythic nighttime haunted stories.

III. Art

1.

The screen is too wide to take it all in
with one view.
No matter how far back you stand,
the mountains,

like gigantic moss-covered
pine cones, lean,
look to be bent askew
by time and wind,

their slopes too sheer
to climb. Move
from panel to panel.
So much is shown

in miniature—-minuscule cranes,
two men poling
two tiny boats
and a thin river slightly widening

as it flows west—-that you think,
culture, a civilization,
tradition, means this:
time intensified, movement stilled.

2.

A solitary duck floats
downstream.
High up, in a wood hut,
two men,

in fluent robes, talk while gesturing,
their aged faces
little more than a few,
quick brush strokes.

In a den of sorts, not quite the mouth
of a cave, a monk sits
chanting, shaded by clouds
and a plum tree trunk.

3.

Turn around. A porcelain bowl
displayed in a case
behind thick glass
is white like robes worn to mourn

a passed soul, pure
as a jade vase
vast age has not changed
save for a swirl

of pale blue around
a thin inner rim—
an almost flat pot
or dish silent, cold as frost.

Some night it might happen, like
a blunt moment
of shock, spirits appearing
to greet you while you sleep. A new

bowl you thought old, whiter
than fresh snow
yet as ancient
in its devotions as a monk

praying in a cave centuries ago,
imagining hands
some far off
day moulding it from his river's clay.

IV. *Love*

Envision it. The body in love embodies the body of love.
The body lives within the soul. Record what you might know of
it. A small beach, its gritty sand brittle as dry grass. A lake
rippling through reeds, slapping against a cement pier
beneath a diving board. A solitary garter snake.
Jasmine. Magnolia. Roses. Whose perfumes belong here
with them now. Houses' lights flickering off the calm water
geese drift on sleepily. White sheets of clouds
masking a waxing moon. A dam, its overflow stirring
the quiet creek below it. What nighttime enshrouds
old age revives. A car door slammed. The humid air
dew-heavy. Their naked bodies like mirrored light, the glow
off gold, the patina on bronze. A late August evening is smiling
down upon them with its usual enticements. What two dare
to do by embracing. Eyes that meet in secret and know why. So
it cannot be paradise. Yet call it grace, beneficence. The shock of love beginning.

The Mothers

1.

The mothers sit on porches, eager for word,
murmuring among themselves. Last night's
lightning, with its fine axe, thunder heard
round the world, split tall trees into timber

it scattered on the ground. A hawk alights
on a roof to signal it's true, the rumor
of ships sinking off the coast. The women
stalk the shore, search for bodies, toss

rose wreaths into the sea. When the men
return from the boats talking of loss
and doom, their wives, refusing to listen,
turn their backs. They know of the dolphins

strewing the beaches, the pigs drowned in
their wallow, the graves dug for the sons
of mercy and its consolations
during the long ago years of perpetual winter.

2.

You have only begun to mourn. Come away,
fellow sailors. In this part of the world,
in this season, when all seems hurled
about, the nights too long, each day

too short, come away. They shouldn't have left
in such bad weather, boys who no longer rest
in their arms. It is the worst theft
of all, their children stolen, the village's best

taken as hostages. In a fable-like story one
mother re-tells, she sits by herself on
her screened porch paring apples, preparing
a pie for her son, squinting, searching

for a skull and cross bone flag flapping over the horizon.
It is an age-old tale of pirates she relates, its message
plain. Their captives lives are hard. They rage
at fate, cry for their mothers. There is no talk of ransom.

The Le Nain Brothers' Adoration of the Shepherds

There's no stable. Instead a ruin more Greek
than Roman. Broken Doric marble columns,
strings of ivy twined or dangling from them
while a donkey impassively waits behind

Joseph. Mary is adoring her baby, meekly
kneeling, her shawl a dark plum-
skin black. No sheep. One cow, nuzzling him,
the swaddled baby whose face looks resigned

to his future fate. An old shepherd
leans on his staff. By his side,
a girl and a younger boy stand, likely his children,
their bodies partially hidden by their father's.

All are silent, worshipful in their way and so word-
less. Two angel children provide
a peek at heaven, the girl in pale pink, not vermillion
like Mary, the boy in drab green, his cloak's colors

identical to the shepherd boy's who wears a hat
like an upside down bowl. He could be the older brother
of the angel. Strangely, neither
looks at the infant, but are staring out of the frame.

At whom? What is so amazing, astonishing to them that
it distracts their gaze from Jesus? A light brighter
than an incarnate god's? What could be a greater
miracle? A glorious something, whatever it is, aflame

in the distance? No matter.
It is an unseen splendor
their eyes direct the viewer
to, and nothing after will ever be the same.

Dare County Cemetery

An ancient cedar grove, a ring
of rose beds round it
in late summer. A rope swing
waiting for a child to sit
in it and play. Wind inspires wind. Sap
drips from a golden ash tree.
A leather strap, a scratched-on scrap
of paper rest ignored on the mossy
soil of the brick-lined cemetery
with its iron gates, marble
headstones, myriad people
lying below the sod, unable to see,
though their soulful eyes open wide
as they sigh, seeking mercy,
a happier place to hide
in from rainstorms, the unending pain
of being dead. Bend an ear
to the ground. Listen
to them whisper. Don't fear
them because they've been forgotten.
Discarded urns, empty vases. Names
and dates erased by time,
the burned out flames
of their lives. What is their crime,
to be denied the grace of your memory,
the ghosts who host each other
for lack of better
among the living of Dare County?

Bayview Cemetery

Grandparents, parents, two aunts, more buried
in our old family tomb overlooking the Hudson.
From the heights, I can watch people being ferried
over the river, though not as it once was done
with coins for the ferryman to carry them
securely across to wherever it was the dead
were meant to go. Mowed grass, soft moss, trim
hedges surround chipped gravestones by the lead-
gray monument to my bloodline's hopes and pride
and folly. Lillies, poppies entwine a boxwood hedge, tall
and green. Charon, look at me. I keep a silver dollar
safe in my pocket or by my bed. Someday, I'll hide
it on my tongue for you to take as payment. To oar me far
as you need to go to make sense of death on the silent other side of the wall.

Bill's Ghost on Paros

i.m. Bill Mayer

It is shortly past sunrise, but no birds are singing,
not yet. It is cold for Greece, the fog, pale white,
slowly receding to the sea, a bitter chill stinging
his eyes as he stares out far past the rising half light.

Off shore winds sound their own mournful music.
He looks down at his young man's hands,
surprised, no doubt a moment's trick
of the mind, after a man has died, no one understands.

How much the wilds of Paros appear to be the same
as the stormy day he left it decades
ago, only hard weather left to tame
mountains, no more wanton gods, pirates, crusades.

So this is where the end has brought him, to the island
where, it is possible, his poetry began,
to the ancient women, black hair sand-
gritty, exposed skin, clothes filthy, crag-faced fisherman

husband bound to the sea's cruelty, harsh life,
men they know one day they will weep
and weep for, a widow, never more a wife,
silently sweeping the tiered white steps, the steep

paths before the white-washed houses while waiting
for them to return, tragedy's
origins, or one of them, in the common pain
of the daily, primordial, the dream the poet sees

as his own, as everyone's, an old woman dressed
head to toe in night black, staring out, out,
beyond sight, far past the horizon, blessed,
alive still, still hoping, ever faithful, ever devout.

Linda's Kore

i.m. Linda Gregg

Perhaps her poems have fulfilled her dreams,
her longings after all and so have become the poet
as much as she who wrote them. Perhaps
they have shown her readers what life meant
her to become: the prayers that survive her.
In them, deer still nip at her precious small breasts
on a hill in west Marin. A yearling nibbles
her golden hair. Though her horse has trotted
away, its beauty quiets her soul. She feels as free
as the love-struck girl she was on Santorini. As unable to stay.

What do her poems revive? The sea. Flayed snakes
seeking dark trees. Whatever might save a spirit
from grief. Why let it all go? Why despair of passion?
Words, images tasting of ripe melons, redolent
of does roaming in woods, shiny as the shawls
of black clad widows washing clothes on rocks,
fated as salmon swimming upstream to spawn.
She has shut her windows to the city's intrusions,
to whatever would make her forget, refuse
her her faith in words' capacity to restore sanctified things.

Sacred as a bowl of brown rice sprinkled with sesame
seeds and soy sauce. Small pleasures that suffice
to remind her, even after she has set her pen
aside for good, what a poem can be when worthy
of the permanent hurt she feels, the wound
of perpetual mourning, the pain of final
things. Yet graced as well with happiness, sudden
laughter like Jack's child-like sighing with delight
over her body in the aftermath of their ecstasy.
Why let mortality obscure either sun or its shadows?

Rejoice in the good you are given. Life sweet as honeyed
almonds, lemon cakes gently frosted.
Moments precious as island breezes, heron fishing in a lake,
fern fronds at twilight, swallows in flight,
her own bright nakedness while bathing under
a moonlight that shines with the same soft
radiance through paneless windows onto the bed
where she and Jack made love each night.
Why permit life, like a man, to shut its doors
on her, lock her in a closet, leaving no way out as he prowls?

Old women must still thresh in the valley east
of the mountain in Paros where she found
the terra-cotta shard of a kore, her kore,
whom she believed to be holier than
Aphrodite, the fragments, head, arms, torso,
she had dug up with her fingers, clawed
for deep into the ground, the girl's headband
wound round the plaited strands of her hair.
She could have watched them forever: the crane
and two white-eyed gulls flying above the olive grove.

Bound to the myth, I say, Let waves shift sand and pebbles
on Kolymbithres' fossil-like granite beach
while the sun-bright sea, dazzling at sunrise,
answers her prayers. Let her glance up at the kore
resting on her shelf in her apartment. What
beauty, Semele-like, has set it on fire today?
She listens intently to the women of the chorus
chanting of the water-bearer, the threnody
poems learn to sing after their poet has died. Untimely
Semele who for her passion burned with the knowledge of god.

Loxias, after a Photograph by Galen Garwood

At Delphi millennia ago, Apollo proclaimed, "All my oracles are liars."
Recall how Daphne fled the sun then, the stag king Actaeon
and his dogs were maddened by the moon. A god's desires
transmute those he adores. Seascape gray, a Mediterranean
storm looms. The light surges like waves. Hera's temple's in ruins.
A city waits anxiously on a hill, a long, crane's neck tower rising
from it like a thin smokestack. Today no one will lose, no one will
win. Neither ancient nor modern ways offer refuge. A boy is dashing
through a field filled with thick, blistered weeds. His own mantle's
been lost or cast aside, and what he wears now is the torn cloak
he was given as a gift from the god whom, wearing baggy pants, he still
must run and run from, out of fear of death and divine possession. A smoky
sky rhymes with the fires burning, raging within him. Apollo will be untrue
to you, it says. Fly from him, though you will lose. Passion outraces you
every time you try to escape his embrace, ever more terrible, ever more beautiful.

Temple Gate

for Robert Mohr

1.

For those like you who must make
it across, the ways of the world
grow more difficult, all temples
strictly closed. The sky glows at dawn
as an old wavy-headed fellow
slowly walks barefoot down the hill
toward the beach, dressed in rags
blotched with mud. The slope is
long and steep. I step away as he
passes by me. His white hair glitters
in the early light. If I did not put this
down on paper who would guess
his need to find his way back home
through wisteria vines and iron gates?

2.

I write these words–swift as a breeze
blows through my windows–to keep
what is fading from fleeting further.
Outside, hawks hungrily circle antennae
on neighbors' roofs. Error is the old
man's monkish gray beard I failed
to mention, the anguish visible on
his face as he bears on his shoulder
the torn, stained comforter in which
he sleeps, the bed he lays out
on a slab of concrete as he huddles
in a doorway until sunrise comes
to hustle him away or noon rages
at his age with its numb, blinding heat.

3.

So vast is the gap between heaven
and earth that no one can say all is
well with us. I close the shutters,
dawn hurting my eyes, gauze curtain
dusty as mist, no promise of cooler
days. I no longer know who I am,
open a window facing the sea
to watch waves break, white capped
as far as the horizon. Do you recall
the basilica we visited once on
our way to L.A.? How we strolled in
its cemetery's garden as an ancient
monk with white curly hair pruned
roses, unfazed, smiling sunward unmindful of danger?

4.

Bright day, then another brighter,
brighter than sun,
brighter than noon,
brighter than vision,
the moon now set, too,
and you and I, lovers,
hiking slowly down
a cliff, a steep slope,
a ravine almost, night
after night as a white
bearded monk keeps us
company, coming, going,
leaving us to wait by a river,
leaving no trace, no map to guide us.

5.

Which way did it face? The dream,
I mean, of an ancient temple gate,
vines dangling from all four
walls, the wind through the ruins
like distant voices chanting, no
proof of anything, of course, hard
to tell where the singing came from
or if anything out there was singing
at all. When a love collapses in
the beat of a heart, it breaks
like an altar relic or sacred tablets
inscribed with fragments of names.
When a faithful soul vanishes, dusk-lit,
it shocks the earth with its absence

6.

Suppose mercy is a white cloud rising over
dry hills, a bird that sings without
yearning for the woods it flew
through, an icy stream we stepped in
hip high, the mysteries of intention.
Suppose it is my confusion of love for
you and the world, that it be no illusion.
You care for your dying aunt thirty seven
hours by plane from your home while
the air everywhere is miasmic, fraught
with danger. Suppose, why not?, the old man,
the ragged man with his comforter slung
over his shoulder, is a down on his luck itinerant
monk, prophetic of days when all the old temples re-open.

Self-Portrait

for Atticus Carr

1.

A bright, vivid May. Thistles growing out of red clay,
ivy-entwined thickets, dogwood, backwoods in shade
and shadows, noon sun untamed, cardinals, a jay,
a scrappy feral cat squabbling with crows, a jade-

like pale green to new leaves and dew-wet grass,
chipmunks, squirrels, oaks' twisting, thick roots,
quick creeks leading to a widening lake, No Trespass
signs posted by half-sunken, rotting rowboats, newts,

tadpoles, minnows. And we, happy, swimming nude
together, lying after on a muddy bank, a strong spring
storm on the way, raindrops large as pebbles, our solitude
oblivious of sorrow, the beautiful promise that comes to nothing.

2.

We were fated never to make love there
again, each to greet the other,
embracing in the meadow, bare-
boned as we now are, my brother.
Say a lake reflects the stride of egrets
as they wade, unmolested, in shallows
where an anchored boat's lights rest
like tired hands upon the water
or, splayed wide, a shed flight feather
while we hunt for what's left of a nest,
its sticks and tiny cracked shells. Cows
low near a weathered fence. Egrets' silhouettes
shade the lake, its calm unbroken by undertows
at twilight as a life of suns sets into the darkening air.

3.

After the rain has stopped, the soaked leaves,
shaken by winds, drip, trickle steadily
onto a forest floor choked
with weeds and brush, fall's foliage heavy
on the ground. In late October, twilight
flickers with a golden gleam deep in woods, fern trees'
fronds shining, dolomite
boulders sparkling, a bright,
glittering creek, moss on stumps and logs,
all luminous till earth gives way to dark. I have looked
far into a woodland's shadows while tree frogs croaked
and owls hooted in a grove. I have listened late at night
to the gentle dripping of leaves. I have lain, sleepless, on a grassy
knoll and heard what nothing sounds like when nothing's all that's left to see.

4.

Yellow birch, red alder, red oak,
white pine, moosewood,
marsh fern, lady slippers,
bluebeard lilies, poke-
berries, toadflax: spring's things, now winter's
to claim for its own as perhaps it should.

Chunks of ice drift down the river. Each day
is colder, darker. The snow's
icy crust crackles. The mossy grass is frozen. Gray
clouds blur the sun. A sharp wind blows
through a thicket of brush and pine
where a rack
of stag's antlers and splinters from a snake's spine
show through the snow cover, bone brittle and muddy black.

5.

I recall a Rembrandt self-portrait of the sad, weary,
agèd man he caught sight of in his mirror when old.
I first saw it at the Metropolitan Museum years ago,
an elderly man from whose eyes shone a light Caravaggio
usually saved for young boys' bodies. A tree
when its leaves are failing in autumn, its bold
yellow gleaming colors stolen from the sun
at noon, can reveal in its way the same
intensity as if inside it there were a flame
burning all the brighter before its day is done.
So why do I wonder if it is true that youth lingers on
in the liminal half-light and growing shadows, dim
as twilight, of my old man's vision? What can I say to him,
the boy I was, smoldering inside me like the embers of dusk just
before night claims its godhead over us both, but I have known love. Stay by me.

Epilogue and Prayer

Swirling winds tear and scatter petals from a garden
behind a wayside inn, a storm
over low lying hills anxious to unburden
itself of its rain, to form
itself into thin white clouds again, drifting
through skies, no longer maddened
by the lightning that gashes the land, the heaving
thunder it is fated to carry inside it, saddened
to have to frighten you: like a man offering again
for you to touch his wounds, oozing, not yet healed,
wanting to let you feel or sense how his pain
is much of who he has come to be, praying if he revealed
his blood-red sores to you you'd come to know it is not sorrow
alone suffering brings, nor is it spring yet either, nor an unknown tomorrow.

May each of us, at the end of our days, be spared
the wrath of our cruelties, the rage of memory's
curse, reminding us of our unkindness, those who cared
for us whom we failed. We, who do only what pleases
us, may we be forgiven for not loving enough,
for achieving only what was convenient,
what desire sought, who believed we could bluff
our way past death and need never repent.
In our last hour, relieve our minds and souls
of our hard words, each unkind, uncaring thing
we've said and done, you, who are music, who sing
in imagination, the angel fable says controls
our final moments, save us as we die, preserve
in our souls the love, the gifts we were given, and didn't deserve.

A Last Hike In, *A Last Look Back*, and *Spare Change for the Crossing* compose a trilogy of books, recollective in several senses and thematically intertwined, which Peter Weltner wrote in his eightieth and eighty-first years. He regards them together as his final book, a kind of culmination of a lifetime of thought and experience. A bit frailer these days than he would like, he continues to live contentedly, if reclusively and out of sorts with the present state of the arts and the perilous condition of the humanities, with his husband, Atticus Carr, by the Pacific.

www.ingramcontent.com/pod-product-compliance
Lightning Source LLC
Chambersburg PA
CBHW020420130626
46549CB00006B/2664